AF265288

I watched, as your fingers
gently stroked
across your chest, arms,
face, laying
still beneath the apple tree,
fruit I wish
to eat, our smiles collide
with intentional
grace, spoken with busy
tongues
of how we will meet

Facebook post a precious
picture pleasing people
today, timeline ticks
together reminding of the
past, life lingers but only for a
bit, post, a distant
dimension, media monger
the you, id and ego,
multiplied by world power,
precious post a pummeled
wave in the sea

Deliver us, this day,
that we may lay
upon our soul, love
repenting and forgiving,
salvation to us that pray,
coached by invisible force
we know and love,
peace be with us, today,
tomorrow,
eternity

You ruin the moment of creative
flow, flow in which it writes,
writing the vision, the picture,
the story, story that takes on,
takes off and validates emotional
undertaking, an undertaking of
pouring emotions, expressed in the
pen, paint, pornographic desires,
shot out of a loaded soul, like
the cum on her face, tits, pussy,
pussy that inspires us all, man
and woman, since dawn, the dick,
the vagina, the want, the need as
a stick to a pool of water, wading,
wondering, thirsty, inspiration
comes from origin, inspiration isn't
a hostage, hostage meets death when
no longer valuable, valuable is
the creative flow, flowing gently
and steadily, when looked upon in
admiration, only to feel comfortable
and get swept under its current,
current that shits you out on the
bank, the dam, the unwanted debris,
where it becomes all for not

I want you so bad, I hear your voice,
     your words, your body, speaks to
my loins, sending blood pumping to
swollen member, I want you so bad,
I feel your lips grace my neck, my
lips, my stomach, engulfing my hard
cock in your wet mouth, I want you
so bad, to touch me gently, feeling
the hairs, muscles, fat, as I gaze
at your beauty, I can feel you want
and love in the form of your pussy,
I want you so bad, my cock enters
you with ease, gliding through your
sweetness, tasting your cum on my
tongue, I want you so bad, I grab
the flesh of your hips in thrust,
buttocks pressed against me, my hand
upon your head pressing it downward,
back arches with each clap of our
rhythm, together we cum in and on
each other, I fill you until overflow,
I want you so bad, I stroke my hard
member, all it's veins and flesh
pleased, cumming on myself, on my
stomach, chest, face, I want you so
bad, my actions are an extension of
you, though afar, I clean myself off
and go back to my beer and television

A boulder, a wall, a mountain in
daylight, you see the space and all
its magnitude
you see yourself, a spec of sand in
the presence of the universe
from dawn to dusk and dawn again,
sightless see and seers seek
in daylight, fear is free, accepted,
respected, hardened wisdom
giving you heaven, giving you hell
when angelic wings falsify
ability to fly, in a second you will
be Icarus in Musee des Beaux Arts,
in daylight, you do not forget,
night sets, blackness blinds the
earth, space, void is you

I struggle with the puzzle piece
It just won't fit
Hundreds of pieces scattered
Clump of piles of color and shape
I twist it and turn it, a square in
a circle
I say fuck it and walk away
several days I return
puzzle piece in front of me fits
it fits, now, next piece
mother fucker!
it doesn't fit
I finish the puzzle, how long, who
knows
all this time for an image of a
cute kitten in a basket of yarn,
next, the trash

Accept/surrender surrender/accept
two factors we must embrace
I am me and you are you
two that will never be one

Surrender to all the fucked up shit
you create and put yourself
through,
quit the bullshit and let it go,
people and things are just that.
determination, strength through
grinded teeth,
your purpose defined without crew,
when truth be told, mind free flows
until you meet the surface below

Alone in bed, the sheets brush
flesh of nipples, hard and stiff
causing jolt of joy from lip to lip
she touches one and then the other
gently playing as fingertips
circle, circle and pull
mind wonders, thinks, debates
and delivers decision, drawer open
in preparation, one hand glides
across
belly, soft, succulent, other
around neck, soft, succulent
legs separate as hand strokes
vertical slit, at first, together
quickly opened blossom of wet
flowering pleasure, fingers
continue to circle, circle, circle
with first rush of passionate wave
drawer introduces a foreign invader
welcomed into the land

Midnight air, crisp
dots blur distant blimp of light
window frames endless centuries
darkness blankets eyes
until consciousness begins its shift

The morrow brings a withered tale
of moi, tattered dreams and
succulent
scenes of screams, moans and wails,
not of Jerusalem or pity
about your day, ones that set sails
from moans down to the bay, where
mouth tastes supple lips, holy grail
of pleasure, fingers, tongue
and love from member,
morrow brings hails
of victory, victory from both sides

Kiss with tongue inserted
tingles, squeezes below
bite on lobes causes love to wet
between massaged breasts with
pinch
sends hips to grind, gyrate
touch to soft belly
opens pathway to sweetness
spreading exposed joy
delivers an ache of pleasure
entering with tip until
eyes widen with mouth agape
firmness
brings pleasure to two and one
at separate same times

Days pass and days end
night is night and day is day
in between is you, you, one
close in thought and in heart
regardless of day or night
or feelings of wrong or right
its truer than anything in this
world
or the next metaphysical play

Noodles slurped as sloppy seconds
before bed so stomach's full
bowl half of hollow globe
tasty shit with chia seeds
pajama top with matted pocket
mattress ready for body comfort
resting eyes while noodles process
awake with sun today is present
fond of the food from bowl to bowel

Glass holds the mother's milk
placed upon your door
taste smooth as orient silk
on body draped du jour
lips part for of that ilk
she drinks it all amour
final drop I try to bilk
her fate for me implore

We sat on the sofa, talking
of this and that and beating
around the bush about others,
we moved to the dining table,
talking of this and that and subtly
inserting comments about others,
in bed we lay, talking of this
or that and finally saying what we
                                feel
about others, then wonder why we
                              waited
       all this time to say it,
as we wake in the morning, tired

Street, lit by candlelight
as curved cars park, parade
perfectly rolling in unison
Delina, kicks the stand up
ignition turns to go
helmet strap and glasses
frame her beauty, she throttles
with scarf pressed against her
breast,
she zooms and zigs between two
vehicles, some side by side
others staggered, lights overhead
flicker faintly, glowing gold
as a spotlight on her life
Delina freely follows her heart
on motorbike, she gets there faster
by zigging like a stardust

Peter hangs on with loose grip
as the ape-hangers guide
his direction, straddled, Peter
chokes back his thought
and air as he kicks with force,
turning over the cold motor,
Delina, bites her lip in
anticipation,
she feels the vibration rattle
her core, she grabs onto his
shoulder
and leaps on the iron horse,
her thighs squeeze as her arms
squeeze his waist, Peter's head
turns and nods,
Delina smiles, riding bitch was
never a thought
until now, now, she wants nothing
more,

the fairing protects from the bugs
and debris
but the wind finds their face,
hugging
their body, the motorbike glides
with tires grip, they lean and
thoughts
disappear as the trees pass in
blurring
bliss, Delina lays her head upon
Peter's back,
words can't travel over noise of
her roar,
words are heard by the warmth of
their love,
Peter, in silence, vows to never let
her become garage rot,
he smiles like he has never smiled
before

She spoke the words I need to hear
the words that speak and draw so
near
near, I hear the words so clear
clearer are the words in mere
of blurring eyes from tears that
cheer
words spoken from her seer
the heart, in me, will never
disappear
said and meant for me right here
and now and forever and a day

The chest, it tightens
the eyes, they sink
the stomach, will ache
the words, are spoken
the truth, unfolds
the ears, are open
the I, let go
the you, released
the me, surrender
the she, believed

I have a thorn deep within me
piercing in agony
I thrash about reckless
driving closest away
thorn grows bigger and deeper
jagged edges slice open
hatred anger fear sorrow
I have a thorn deep within me
watershed of known and unknown
origin
piercing in agony
I double over from the hurt
that love causes as it is expelled
to the surface

My heart sinks when you say
the things you say, directly,
with a bite of harshness, then
sorrow fills my beating heart,
like the pendulum that cuts flesh,
so does your words, my heart sinks
when you say my words are impure,
wrongful intentions, pics become
voyeur disgust, my heart sinks,
filling me with questions, questions
of doubt, about you, about me

Scales glide across a wasteland of
love
dunes pile and peak, ever changing
landscape of romantic embrace
feet sink in struggling steps
imprint made with force to be
washed over by soft breeze
as if never made
sun shines bright as halo burns
head
a dune that was always in front of
you
welcomes you to climb and see
babylonian oasis with shade trees
and a pool to caress your lips
and bath you with love

She wipes the glass, beers aligned
neatly
bottles and cans, Beck influenced
beat
a buck, a dollar, a finite tip
if it ain't where it's at
we take the pointer from the
sisters
tables don't clean themselves
piss on floor, shit in toilet
end of the night, a glorious moment
for you and you and you
to get the fuck out!

On the road
or off the grid
in suburbia or
in the city
out on the prowl
or prowling around town
cruising for a bruising
rolling deep on dubs
donuts in the yard
peeling out in the street
treading lightly on trails
through hiking on foot
regardless,
I watch the direct, indirect,
instant, lengthy, one word
or 500 message
do this ......

From Mayberry to murderer
Gooooooooooollllllyyy I'll kill a
mother fucker!
I walked the streets and served the
community
from garage to sheriff to Vietnam
the divided nation I'll burn their
shit down
I come home to Mt. Pilot, now a
forgotten village
made a laughingstock
30 years later by Kubrick, fuck
him
I'm mother fucking USMC, get some!

Brutus smiles with elegance, grace
before the courts and after defeat
he smiles with elegance and grace
Pompeii or Pompey who the hell
                                knows
Brutus of Younger, story is old
                                 news
you lost your war and killed a
                                 hero
this is the only recognition you'll
                                  get

I profess my love on a canvas
keyboard
to you, you, the one, who speaks an
angelic tongue
whipping winds a quilted embrace
natural, as two beasts, calling in
the night
bamboo sways a dance for us
barks give us a cheer
my fingers brush the hair from
your face
blood flows hot a radiating heat
torch glows blue
until the world can travel in waves
my screen is you

I sit alone and wait by my phone
no ring nor vibrate or flashing of
                                light
letters printed that sail the waves
   my head hangs and stretches my
                                 neck
eyes draw to thumbs, extension of
                                 mind
     everything spoken sits in the
                     triangular void
of waters deep, I navigate
          into rocks, my words
          begin to fill my vessel,
                        I drown
due to my lack of cosmic navigation

Rope pulls tight in knotted delight
wrapped, looping cords over under
are hands above, behind, praying
for love
does it matter when legs are apart
thrusted, busted, delighted and
disgusted
across the neck and one full of
hair
screams, cries, moans and ties
today, tomorrow, expand on the lie

Trust the lust, avoid the bust
open the door, lay on the floor
insert your member, piles of timber
spread the secret, mythic
discreetness
vulnerable and pleasant, explosive
decadence
trust the lust, avoid the bust
and life will be a fucking gift

You know what you know and there
is no solution other than the one
you know
right is right when it goes in your
favor
answer your own question when the
question you ask is not the correct
question
trust your gut unless its upset
then just remember that feeling
pay attention to the important
things that are important to you
but may not be important to others
don't look at another woman or
man unless your woman or man is
ok with you looking but don't look
like you want to look or look to
long because staring is rude
you have a good sniffer but don't
sniff woman's or men's hair or
other things attached unless they
say it is ok to sniff them

keep it in your pants unless it is
not there then keep it between your
legs unless it's time to show it
you can only have a taste, just
not too much of a taste, depends on
what your tasting and is it worth
tasting
when you have a taste, balance your
gaze, sniffing then pull it out and
trust your gut and fuck it

Portal open to an opposing
dimension
tree limb cracks, breaks and falls
sucked into a backyard well
of unprecedented, unrefined swirl
the other side of God knows
but do you? Portal spins, pulses,
pounce
trip over a broken branch and poof!
fucked off into in infinite abyss

She looks at me!
Does she look at you?
Is it with one or two?
Does it matter?
I don't know!
I'm staring at her cleavage!
SEX!!!
With a woman or man
Whose ever tits are bigger!

Love of the craft, my pen the
amulet of Cthulhu
Chant: (We Samasathiti for you)
Worshiping a language, unspoken by
tongue
Chant: (Tongue of Ten Fingers)
Older than Gilgamesh's ancient
relatives
Chant: (We cannot relate to your
time)
Invisible world visible to world
Chant: (What it is is now to be)
Your world and mine!
Chant: (We all adhere to it)
It is written
Chant: (We are of it now)

The bar spans empty seat between
me and all, laughter and obnoxious
glee fills the air with noise, I sit
smashed between old and young
drunk
swaying, bumping, leaning into me
but I stay focused, on drink, and
composure
before my knuckles connect with
nose, eye
and chin, then, I sleep it off
behind bars

Seconds tick forward then back
hands wave red flags, only
annually
atomic scientists with personalities
of assholes, snapping their fingers
to the beat of the jazz band of
death
global climate change, fall of
mankind
bombs not fucking flowers, atomic
scientists
make bombs, NASA Nazi nice guy
Jesus reminded us who his father
was
constantly, maybe a little prayer
would do us good, then watching a
clock
that doesn't tell time tell me what
time
it is

Movie reels play timeless pieces
time may be dated but masterpieces
nonetheless, a dramatic sunset
or confusing sequence, we watch
compelled to be in the world
emotional connection disconnected
from reality, the reel keeps
rolling
there will never be an end, only
a need to relive the stories we
know
until no more

White paper, clean edges, sharp
sliced finger, more painful than
the knife
in pocket, stinging, throbbing
hand uses fingers to grasp pencil
waving, tracing, shading, connecting
thought to image, swirls develop
waves of something from nothing
cut reminds the finger it exists
just an empty appendage, connected
to the greater hand of
righteousness
white paper, now a shade of coal
with smears from palm, the image
feels
incomplete, unfinished, the thought
cannot be contained to this frame,
no,
boundaries can be contained, the
blemished
white paper is flipped to be white
again

Boredom bears a big burden
beyond the brains and brawn
before your brilliant ideas
and after your boo hoos
lies a big big problem
you

Each strike given and taken
release of my wrong doings
every strike that is laid upon me
each blow that I consume
is the whip upon my back to repent
I strengthen my body to be the
whip
I strengthen my mind to accept my
beating
remembering it is you that deserve
what you bring to the world
and the weak will crumble to dust

I sit alone in the bar
staring at everyone from afar
no conversation, no one to touch
just me and my stool and a punch
from the shot that burns my throat
dead and a trip on the boat
rocky river I float
to the cries and screams of black
goats

She sits in silence as still as a
painting
locks parted by her sea of strands
each perfectly placed around her
face
sparkles reflect images of me
I sit in silence mesmerized by her
presence
each collapse of my lungs expels
my soul
journeying closer towards her
parted lips
I watch as her tongue glides over,
moisturizing
her labium inferius oris, imperfect,
slightly
skewed left to right, yet, perfectly
placed on a goddess

Bed burrows my soul
building a blanket fort around me
blowing bliss into my eyes
breaking my sight until darkness
bleeds beautiful images of things
I want or don't want, until it's
there
woman, sensual, bellowing bawdy
for me, to be between her breathe
and her breast, downwards I drudge
bordering below her naval, tasting
nectar, softened skin
sensation summons serendipity
boasting big breathtaking blows
from my lips to hers

Motivation inspiration constipation
stop
deviation manipulation evaporation
stop
derivation hesitation desperation
stop
perforation exasperation political
nation stop
your wall my wall their wall not
green hills rolling hills dusty
hills stop
cut the wire stop
pull the trigger stop
dottie dot dot dot stop
fuck your message...

I left the house. Evening was early.
Walking, cars passed on their way
home, others passed on their way
to an early dinner. I had a couple
hours before the sun set. My pace
was slow and awkward. I always
felt awkward walking, and this
was no different. Feet seemed to
project me forward; yet, always
out of sync. Everyone driving by
watched as I clumsily staggered
along. The feeling made me angry
and sad. I pulled my cap tight and
low, straightened my back, tucked
hands away and walked. As I pass
through the neighborhoods, I ducked
between two homes as a short cut.
Over the years, my feet wore the
path. From concrete to open fields.
I felt relaxed. No one, no cars, no
spirit to hear my tears. I lit a
cigarette and sat for a bit. It was
still early. In the field, I felt
secured yet vulnerable. I could see
for miles all around. I could see
them coming but they could see me
as well.

I would be able to get the jump
on them because I was waiting for
them. So, I made myself small.
All you could see is the puff of
smoke lingering in my presence.
As the sun began to settle, I
decided to continue. Past the field,
I found myself back in society.
Gas stations, busy intersections
busy, speeding vehicles. I run out
in front of one relying on my
keen sense of distance. Alive, I
stop at my local shop for a pack
of smokes. I slam the pack with
purpose into my palm. The tobacco
tightens like a magic trick. Like
a present, I unwrap the cellophane
and pull one out. As I lite and
inhale, I become another person.
I swing the door open like an old
western. The light sprays the room
and all you see is a haze and faces
staring at the intruder. I walk to
my table acknowledging no one. I
place my jacket on the back of my
chair and quarters neatly in a row
on my table. I walk over to the
wall filled with cues and pick the
crookedest one.

Squatting down, two quarters enter
the slot, with force I push in and
then it pushes back. The sound
of release as balls fall in line.
Strip, solid, strip, solid. Perfect
triangle. Tight. I stand on the
other end with confidence as I send
a loud crack that echoes the entire
room.

I sat at the bar
tears carved a groove
as I thought about my son
at an age when blinked
everything changes
and I'm not there

She sits on the bed
folding and crumbling on the edge
her red shoes touch the picnic
patterned
comforter, I wished she'd take them
off
shoes are dirty, walking along the
streets
bird shit, spit and piss, now in
your bed
waiting to transcend on a passing
ship
from the stratosphere
but you can still not be a fucking
filthy
animal in the meantime

Heart speaks for you to listen
we forget about all the wisdom it
has
days struggle to pull us from one
end
to another our heart reminds
us of our purpose
draped in a cashmere robe
on the silk road presented
if we choose to follow

The pen scratches ink stained
words neatly on straight lines of
a white sheet of paper. The hand
that moves the tip across the page
leans and folds into itself with
a delicate grip of confidence. Arm
bends angular arch allowing the
hand to effortlessly glide to and
from while smudging the words into
the blade of the palm. The hand
knows not what the arm does which
knows not what the words say. The
eye doesn't see the image; rather,
the eye sees neatness of the words
size, length, and judgement of
distance to the end of the trail.
The eye guides the hand and arm
to do its bidding, but the bidding
was conjured by the mind as it
percolates around a cauldron. For
the eye doesn't see what is not
written beyond the lines. The mind
writes the words and formulates
the sentence before a drip from
the pen. Controlling the flow and
speed in which it will be read.
Expressing the idea in a language
understood.

The question becomes who controls
the mind. Where does this, these
words, this sentence and the
compulsion to write it come from.
All have a greater thing that
controls the essence of life. The
flower to the bee, the bee to the
honey, the honey to our mouths,
our mouths to our digestion, our
digestion to our nourishment, our
nourishment to our sustainability,
our sustainability to our life,
our life to our work, our work
to our purpose, our purpose to
our community, our community to
our culture, our culture to our
humanity, our humanity to our
planet, our planet to our milky way,
our milky way to our universe, our
universe to our higher power, our
higher power to our mind, and so
the story goes. Here, at this moment
in time, the pen writes the minds
voice and asks us "is this truth?"
"Is this the explanation to how life
must be?" The answer is no. The
answer is the words on the page
are words murdered by the universe
since the first sprout of grass or
drip that became the ocean.

We are all just the drip of water
in an ocean of drops seeking each
other for completion. These words
and all others formed are stolen
from those that have stolen before.
We regurgitate philosophical
phrases to confuse us from the
simplicity of truth which is always
around us. The universe vibrates
the OHM to me, shaking my soul
through a pen. When the vibrations
cease, and the ink well dry, life is
met with void, and in that void will
blossom the realization that will
never degrade. These words act as
my Teflon existence with the idea a
single molecule of myself will find
its way into the universe, to the
higher power, and into your mind,
and then, and only then, will life
be answered and complete.

She licks the stamp and sticks it
on the card, each lick lingers
her finger presses firmly
on each postage, small square
placed on the right white box
she licks and places another
with two fingers she spreads the
creases
out, rubbing it smoothly, ensuring
it is in its right place, breeze
blows
and stiffens her nipples, the lick
of the stamp arouses an event

The light turns on and lens focus
silence, pause, breath, a smile
glow burns blush
on her cheeks, giggles vibrate
radiance all around, time elapses
with no cares, her mind transfers
beyond the clouds, warm tingle
travels
from lips, pulsing her base root
legs squeeze, hips shift, she
permeates all space, feeling grows
her sacral activated, pressing upon
the fifth

She sighs slightly with acceptance
heavy chest pumps in rhythm
controlling the tempo, her hand
rubs
her neck and finds her lips, a
rapid force
she holds the edges, tremendous
scream
internal, reddens face, her eyes
wide,
mouth gape, a pleasant smell of
volatile
liquid drips from her source, now
the world
will use their third eye

My augur speaks in present tongue
her clairvoyance reaches beyond my
                            grasp
a voice within me sings a song sung
guiding me all the while rasped
I'm polished with love and
                righteous incantations
no mysticism, hex or negative
                conjuring
rather, the truth that spells your
                disassociations
with the truest of you and all that
                is alluring
in each breath is a flame scorching
                my soul slow
on a stake, I am tied, subject to my
                inconsistencies
desperately trying to avoid the
                harmonizing control
vibrating my tuner to change my
                frequencies
when complete, I am obliged to
                behoove
forever, now, forward I move

The many different readers
read your every move
navigate, one by one
still you feel removed
they ask and they want
to take you in the tent
scared and nervous
you begin to repent
I have a savior, I have the one
and off you went
for the one you seek
is in the wee hours, sent
back to the site
seeking guidance from within

Explosive encroaches enemy
entertainment
fearing fragments fighter's flea
flocking
germane geographically jerry-
rigging gadgets
hoping half-heartedly horrendous
hell
illicit erroneous ill-intentions
jolting joules justifying
jurisdiction
kill caringly collateral carcasses
clinging
love lingering later

Time Check
my eyes bat lashes untangled
from deepest sleep and dream
my cock is full, hard, pressing
against the mattress, I remember
dream of me going down on you
you, screaming from orgasm
then I wake alone
with a hard cock and it's only
7:20 in the morning

Moments of doubt
coupled with clout
time ticks with request
distance between overzealous
age never dictates
love regardless of state

Dew douses, drips from blades
she wakes with big breath
smell of pollen and pine
fills her biological beautiful body
tent heavy from condensation
river flows, standing in a steady
stream
always in a different place
locusts loudly lament existence
she smiles as she unzips herself
to relieve herself from confinement
and urinate on a tree

I listen
about all the exes in Texas
I don't live in Tennessee though
I live in Texas and I see them
at the grocery store, the mall
the park, on the road
and I smile every time
because I fucked them all

I see your art on flat canvas
sitting perfectly still
it conjures up thoughts
about my head laying
in its place as your fingers
comb the silhouette of my
face and I my arms are warmed
by your embrace

She sings a song that sings the
breeze
inhaled and circulating within my
inner
roads that traverse her warmth
she speaks in speeches that
illuminate
neurons flickering in my mind
which fire
cylinders pumping fuel for her
engine
she is a feeling in me, a feeling
of love
that flows like the river over her
feet
taking part of her wherever it
empties
she is Sofia, Varna, Plovdiv
she is the Danube and the Black Sea
she is Sunny Beach and the coast
she is the trinkets and the shells

I drop the mug, shattered, I look
menacingly
I grab the other mug, filled, I look
complete
I bump my knee on the end table,
bruise
table is now aligned with couch,
content
the sun sets and it's dark and
lonely
sun rises to say I'm here all day
with you

I sleep and arm gets tangled
under head outstretched cocked
lost in dreams of climbing rocks
and kissing lips, to wake
with a dead arm that can't even
wipe my eyes

Schopenhauer, bitter and ugly
philosophically and personally
love is the truest of senses
Hawking's wife to strip club
ventures
knowledge beyond the stars
fairs nothing to love of a woman
man, or whoever your heart
desires, for without love
life is a purposeless pit
of gloom and doom

Until we meet, physical connectivity
derives emotional symmetry
our unity, uncertain chemistry
is always there, mental brevity
sea to sea, transcendental
camaraderie
forever blessed, existentially

The stars shine in kitchen
constellation time glowing shimmer
of existence, unknown distance
space
between me and them, still
the darkest matters bellow
a recognition regardless
of your involvement
and proximity, kitchen time
glimmers hope for your
time on earth

Unison riding wild waves
thrusts us forward backward
till complete collapse

A limp with impeding lisp
A crutch with seceding grip
A patch with protruding tip
A heart with continuous drip
A sorrow with stabbing imp
A speech with stuttering contempt
A life with everlasting despair
Forever doomed by you
Me

Spirals spiral for a reason
the conch shell sings sea songs
bourbon burns away blowing blues
railroad went underground
rifle site set sites singular spiral
out the bourbon barrel into
an unwanted heap
of a worthless cage bird

Words across the page
provide a cold gage
of interpretive emotional sage
but a voice, provides mage
leaving the room to engage
love recently spoken

Time began with no other thought
          struggles of understanding
          interpretation of language
              fading as a cloud pass
one side feels another wondering
      the other side's reciprocation
unknown is eagerness protruding
                  from the source
source is the essence of existence
                birthed from love

Source speaks from within but only
to you
Source known not only to me
expelled open transfer, epitome
of vulnerability, from the doctrine
decree
when the rib joined missing piece,
glee
was rib upon the source, calling
devotee
forever written, source seed
planted delicately
rib's source outstretched,
painstakingly
for her that may never be

Lingering lurking pussy
soft sensual fur
touching gently fingers over
body arch and purring is pussy
when in need of attention
playful exhibition ensues

Nerves and anxiety filled
my being, and your voice whispered
surety, you, woman of calming
presence, immediate trust in you
as I sailed into calm shores

The pawn on the board disposable
tactics pitting pawn against mighty
hopes of triumph overlooked in
movement
rookie only snatches low hanging
fruit
as king's castle switcheroo
when tipped and over all walk away
with pawn to rebuild another losing
battle

I leaned over to pet the frail dog
with ferocity, he sank deep into my
forearm
eyes bitter and filled with hate
he let go and drew back with angry
caution
before pain came shock, my
tenderness
to stroke the gentle creature met
with cold
cruelty, everyone in the room froze
as witness
"O, you can't pet him, he is mean
because my kids beat him,"
I, held back the tears until the
blood trickled
down my forearm and the room
burst in laughter,
feeling ashamed for my weakness
I cried as a child cries when filled
with embarrassment
and realization that you will grow
beaten just as the dog was

She is the crown jewel of
Edinburgh, high above the
Arthurian throne, her gaze grazes
the hilly countryside leading us in
our destiny, spectacles frame her
vision of the sea, guiding us in
flight, homeward, on winged sails

On this day, I thee wed
and it was the greatest moment
second to the moment I saw you
standing in the cafeteria
third to the birth of our baby
all involving you
when I was at my angriest
you met me with love
when I sank deeper
you threw the line
in moments of doubt and despair
you held my hand
you correct my wrong and ground
me
when I live in fantasy
without you I would be lost

Missing the belief and
encouragement
I needed to continue
without you I'd be poorer than what
I am
because I'd never experienced love
that flows from you
as we move the life and into new
journeys
I think about how lucky I am to
have found
my truest mate and mother to our
baby
a feeling many never experience
and we
have 100-fold
I know you will love our second
wife
just as much

First when we wake
before our teeth are cleaned
bathroom splashes urine fountains
hair matted, eyes gobbed shut
that moment, known
to you
to me
beauty of the grotesque
forever and a day

My entire life, I am driven to take
a vow of silence, I want to shut out
exposure and vulnerability
awkwardness of verbalizing me
epitome of existence
as a child, I lacked discipline to
the craft
as an elder, my silence is easily
met
with a dirt nap

Self Portrait
(Response to David Whyte)
What does your belief in a god
or gods matter about your feelings,
a self-portrait doesn't show
the consequences of love and the
pain
that follows with rejection, a self
portrait
doesn't t share with the audience
that living
with the pain is unbearable, you
say you
want to know, but you don't, if you
did, you'd hear your absurdity
at its finest, emptying yourself
to another and rejected, is a death
sentence without a trial

With clenched jaw
heart beats to the fear
without knowing
without seeing
it consumes you beyond
anything known
anything that exists
world spins faster
pressed against the wall
unable to move or resist
only to submit
with clenched jaw
teeth begin to shatter

Authenticity heard in a voice
which rang true to the ear
a gift of honesty to bear
what is closest to the soul
love for you

Save the sermon for someone else
talked at, to, down, degrading
piercing bricks of criticism with
thick
layers of hardened hate, until
impenetrable wall blocks bullets
from entering the soul, soulless
eyes see the congregation with
contempt
as each find their way to hell

A face in stare, out a window
she looks, from nowhere comes
everything, childhood until now,
passed as fast as lined trees and
telephone poles, cheeks redden
blush rose bloom, watered by her
tears as river empties to the sea,
a soft tune hummed that beats an
unbearable feel, drive says goodbye
to end of road, heading back to a
place she wishes would not exist,
tears flow falling, searching for
the stream to carry her homeward

She trickles a stream of least
resistance flowing and fondling the
bed below on her path of grandeur
dreams navigating the world she is
around drip drops dip on through
debris from mother's children
visiting along the way to puddle
conversations filled with love she
moves onward growing along the
way once a little trickle of stream
now the woman of a river becomes
attention from man, good and bad
harnesses her power trafficked for
her beauty
confined she sits silently still in
a pool from her tears until the
day she is able to escape and run
violently to the sea

The world as told from inside this
room,
blown together by salted waves as
told to me from a force within,
shifting furniture freely
Qi ship shapes us and shapes and
ships us off and all over,
as I sit within
polarity of negativity left room
for the positivity of her, her, she
who moves in
at this moment,
precious moment, moment perfectly
timed for us
allowing that which blew my room,
opening sky for ray's warmth dial
pulled you to me,
you, which is me and me, which is
you
together in our room within the
world within ourselves

I adjust my glasses that allow for
me to peer into the convex world
                  within worlds
                  within worlds
she comes to me from the south,
each listening to that whisper
                        within,
two hands become four, energized
forces of touch, tracing sources
sources from above, below, from
      truth at its absolute source
our room, grows before our eyes,
      our space becomes the world
shadow of us, is us, works for us,
      with light of us, that is us

We absorb root from our bottom,
bare flesh, bare soul, purest
penetration
two empresses of this room within
this world, never shying away
making the uncomfortable
comforting, allowing sensation
swallow sensitivity
sensitive are they, to us, outside

Blown is the northwesterly wind,
their sails set with compass zeroed
to their magnetic self
bound to the port city of the
lowlands

www.ingramcontent.com/pod-product-compliance
Lightning Source LLC
Chambersburg PA
CBHW061028050726
47592CB00004B/1378